# AMAZING ASSEMBLIES

## FOR PRIMARY SCHOOLS

### 25 SIMPLE-TO-PREPARE EDUCATIONAL ASSEMBLIES

MIKE KENT

Crown House Publishing Limited

www.crownhouse.co.uk

Published by

Crown House Publishing

Crown Buildings, Bancyfelin, Carmarthen, Wales, SA33 5ND, UK

www.crownhouse.co.uk

and

Crown House Publishing Company LLC

PO Box 2223, Williston, VT 05495

www.crownhousepublishing.com

British Library of Cataloguing-in-Publication Data

A catalogue entry for this book is available from the British Library.

Print ISBN 978-178583069-3
Mobi ISBN 978-178583118-8
ePub ISBN 978-178583110-2
ePDF ISBN 978-178583111-9

LCCN 2016935139

Printed and bound in the UK by
Bell & Bain Ltd, Thornliebank, Glasgow

# CONTENTS

This one is for Jake.

# Introduction

A school assembly for primary children should be exciting and interesting; a time when children can learn, share and contribute to a valuable learning experience.

And that's where this book comes in. *Amazing Assemblies for Primary Schools* consists of twenty-five very special teacher-led assemblies for head teachers, deputies, senior leaders or anyone who is required to lead an assembly with young children at short notice. All the assemblies have been tried and tested, they are all ideal for presenting to large groups of children in the school hall, and they cover a range of subjects. There are science experiments, art demonstrations with unusual materials, word games, puzzles, quizzes, mathematical trickery, even an extraordinary eggshell and a baffling banana!

All the assemblies are interactive, using between two and ten children as 'helpers'. Each one also has a theme which can be developed afterwards in many different ways if children or teachers wish to take up the suggested ideas. The assemblies have been designed with the busy teacher in mind, and although extremely entertaining (and often quite amazing!) they are really simple to prepare. One, for example, doesn't need anything more complex than a pair of scissors and a few sheets of paper, and yet it is guaranteed to fascinate the children watching it.

Once they have participated in these assemblies, it is very likely that the children will want to try the ideas in class or at home, which is a further bonus. Some of the puzzles, for example, can be made easily and will keep the children entertained and amused for hours. Some of the assemblies are more complex than others, so it is always worth rehearsing them before introducing them to the children, especially those involving experiments.

This is an ideal resource book for teachers and leaders in a primary school. All the assemblies are carefully described and the instructions for each are simple to follow. The text is fully illustrated with diagrams and pictures. I hope you and your children get a great deal of enjoyment from them.

# THE EXTRAORDINARY EGGSHELL

## WHAT IS THIS ASSEMBLY ABOUT?

Ask anyone to name some fragile objects and an eggshell will probably feature somewhere on the list. In this session, you demonstrate that an eggshell is far stronger than anyone would believe!

## WHAT YOU'LL NEED:

- Half an eggshell
- Four shapes made from stiff card: a circle, a triangle, a square and a rectangle
- A table
- A pile of hardback books, roughly the same size (for the best effect, the books should be about 30 x 20 cm and about 1 cm thick)
- A small block of wood, the same height as the eggshell half
- If possible, a few pictures of bridges that show circular or triangular shapes in their construction

## PREPARING THE ASSEMBLY

The eggshell will need to be prepared carefully. Crack an egg as evenly as possible and keep one half (save the other half if you want to do two demonstrations). Using a pair of scissors, trim around the jagged edge so that the eggshell sits neatly on the table. Make sure the whole edge is in contact with the surface so, if it isn't, do a little more judicious trimming.

The shapes you will need should be constructed from stiff card. Insert brass fasteners that push through and fold back (as shown in Diagram 1) into the corners of the triangle, square and rectangle.

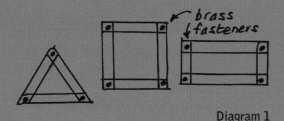

Diagram 1

# Introducing the assembly

**Part 1:** Explain that shapes, as well as having different characteristics, have different strengths. Get two children to come out to the front. Ask them to face each other, hold their hands up and then link hands. They should now try to push each other backwards. The rest of the children should watch what happens to their feet. As the two children 'dig in' to avoid being pushed backwards, they will move their feet apart, forming a triangle with their bodies. If the children watching can't see this clearly, explain what is happening.

**Part 2:** Show that you have made some two-dimensional shapes from some card. Grasp the sides of the square, and pull it into a diamond, showing that the shape can be changed or contorted easily. Do the same with the rectangle. Then show that this is not possible when you grasp the circle or the triangle. These are much stronger shapes, and for this reason are often used in building bridges where strength and stability is needed. Show any pictures or photos you might have.

**Part 3:** Explain that when a shape is curved and three dimensional it is even stronger. Show the eggshell and ask the children whether they think it is a strong object or a delicate and weak one. They will undoubtedly say it is a weak one. Now place the eggshell on the table and, to its left – about 25 cm away – place the small block of wood. Carefully rest the book on the wood and the eggshell, creating a 'bridge'. Place another book on top of the first one and then a third. Ask the children how many books they think the 'bridge' will hold before the eggshell breaks and the bridge collapses. Most will probably say about seven. Add one book at a time, deliberately building up the tension. Everybody will be amazed at just how many books the bridge will hold.

# And finally ...

When the bridge eventually gives way under the strain, explain that it's the shape of the eggshell that gives it its strength. Although the weight of the books is concentrated on one small area of shell, the curved shape means the pressure is actually distributed across a relatively large area. The eggshell is indeed very strong! Perhaps the children can design some other simple but strong bridges and bring them into another assembly.

# Colourful Computation

## What is this assembly about?

Numbers are great things to play around with – often with surprising results. This assembly uses coloured paper squares and, starting with just two colours, shows how rapidly colour permutations grow as more colours are added.

## What you'll need:

Packs of coloured gummed paper squares are a popular item for artwork in primary schools, and you will need four packs, each of a different bold colour – red, yellow, blue and green. If these aren't available, you'll need to cut out some squares of coloured card, the sides of each measuring approximately 12 cm, so they can be easily seen from the front by all the children. You'll need twenty-four pieces of each colour.

## Preparing the assembly

This assembly is very straightforward and is ideal for the occasion when you don't have much time for preparation. Place a strip of masking tape in a straight line on the floor and then put two chairs, each a different colour, say a blue one and an orange one, on the masking tape line. Put the four packs of coloured paper squares on a small table and you're ready to start.

# Introducing the assembly

**Part 1:** Show the children that you've placed two chairs in front of them, and ask them how they are different. You will immediately be told they are different colours. Mention that the blue chair is on their left and the orange one is on the right. Ask a child to come to the front and arrange the chairs in a different way but still keeping them on the masking tape. The child will probably rearrange the chairs so that the blue chair is on the right and the orange chair on the left.

Move the chairs aside and ask another child to come to the front as well. They should stand next to each other on the masking tape line. Give one child a blue square and the other child a red square. Ask them how many ways there are to rearrange the colours. They will say two – either the red can be on the left and the blue on the right, or vice versa.

**Part 2:** Ask a third child to come to the front, and give them a yellow piece of card. Ask the children how many combinations they think there are using three colours. This isn't too hard to work out and a lot of children will probably come up with the correct answer: six. Ask the three children at the front to arrange themselves into the combinations: BRY, BYR, YRB, YBR, RYB, RBY.

**Part 3:** Now tell the children that you actually have four different colours of card, and ask if they can guess how many combinations there might be using this number of colours. A lot of children will probably guess between twelve and eighteen. Point to a child and ask them to come out to the front, pick up one each of the four colours and hold them up in front of every-body. It might, for example, be RYBG. Ask another child to come out and hold up a different combination, which might be GYBR. Carry on in this way. Eventually there will be a lot of children at the front and it will become harder and harder to spot which combinations haven't been done yet. This is great fun and the children will enjoy it. They will be very surprised when they find that just four colours can make twenty-four combinations!

# And finally …

Explain to the children that there is a simple mathematical rule for working out how many combinations can be made from a chosen number of colours. Go over what has been done in the assembly and a few of the children may realise that you need to multiply the numbers together (e.g. 4 x 3 x 2 x 1 = 24). Tell them you will offer a prize for the first child to use a calculator to work out how many combinations there are using ten colours. They'll be amazed to find there are well over 3 million!

# THE CLEVER COIN

## WHAT IS THIS ASSEMBLY ABOUT?

These days we are surrounded by a bewildering variety of products which help to keep our homes clean. But using just two simple and cheap everyday commodities, you can create a most amazing liquid cleaner!

## WHAT YOU'LL NEED:

- A large lemon
- A knife
- Some table salt
- Half a dozen 1p or 2p coins – the older and dirtier the better!
- A saucer
- A teaspoon
- A small dish of warm water
- A box of tissues
- About ten products that are used for cleaning and polishing in the home

## PREPARING THE ASSEMBLY

On the table at the front of your assembly hall, lay out the cleaning products so that the children can see them all clearly. Try to use as large a range as possible – creams, sprays, pads for saucepans, etc. Keep the other materials to the side for the moment.

# Introducing the assembly

**Part 1:** Talk to the children about the importance of keeping ourselves and our homes as clean as possible. Explain how difficult it was to keep things clean in the past. Describe domestic cleaning in Victorian times, for example, and the equipment we now have in modern homes that didn't exist then. Ask the children to describe some cleaning products found in their own home and how they are used, and then make a list of them.

**Part 2:** Talk about the cleaning products you have on the table and ask the children if they can guess what kind of job each one would be used for. Demonstrate a spray polish and show how it cleans, shines and often makes a surface smell pleasant too. Show how a saucepan can be cleaned quickly with a steel wool pad soaked in soap. Talk about the prices of some of the cleaners, and then tell the children that cleaning materials are often composed of quite simple chemicals, plus the addition of water, colourings and fragrances. Explain that you're going to show them the cheapest – and one of the most effective – cleaners in the world!

**Part 3:** Ask two children to come to the front. Ask one of them to place the coins in the saucer and hold it up so everyone can see how dirty they are. The second child should now shake salt all over the coins, until they are covered. Now cut the lemon in half and squeeze lemon juice over the coins as well. Ask the second child to take the teaspoon and stir the coins around for a few moments in the mixture.

Now take the coins out of the mixture and drop them into the small dish of warm water. After a moment or two, take them out and dry them on a piece of tissue. When you hold them up, the children will be amazed to see that the coins look as if they've just been minted!

# And finally ...

Technology changes so rapidly, so ask the children to talk to their grandparents and find out how they cleaned their houses, what cleaning agents they used and what products and equipment were available to them. This kind of 'living history' will reinforce the idea that the world was a very different place even a relatively short time ago. It should also provide some interesting ideas for a good follow-up session during which the children can talk about what they have discovered.

# The Baffling Banana

## What is this assembly about?

You introduce the idea of a vacuum by removing some of the air from a bottle, and then you use this to skin a banana in a very unusual way!

## What you'll need:

- A banana
- Two glass milk bottles, or bottles with necks slightly smaller than the diameter of the banana
- A few strips of paper
- Some matches
- A small orange

## Preparing the assembly

This demonstration can be a little messy so you might want to practise it a couple of times beforehand. Do it on an easily cleanable surface! The inside of the bottles should be clean and dry. At the start of the assembly, sit the orange beside one of the bottles.

## Introducing the assembly

**Part 1:** Show the children the bottle and the orange sitting beside it, and ask one child to come to the front. Then say that you're going to ask her to do something that seems impossible, but isn't. Ask the child to pick up the bottle and the orange at the same time. Everyone will think this is a very easy task, and the child will pick up the orange with one hand and the bottle with the other. Put the orange and bottle back on the table and say, 'Now pick up the bottle and the orange, but you can only use one hand!' The child will think for a moment and will then (no doubt prompted by the other children) balance the orange on top of the bottle and pick up both with one hand. Now say, 'Do it again, but this time you must pick up the bottle and the orange *without touching the bottle.*' The children will quickly say that it is impossible.

**Part 2:** Say that it is possible, but that you're going to need some matches and a piece of paper. Light a paper strip, drop it into the bottle and quickly sit the orange on the bottle neck, pressing it gently. The flame will burn up some of the air, a vacuum will be created and the orange will 'stick' to the bottle, so that both can be lifted easily. Describe what you have done and what a vacuum is. Explain that although the vacuum was trying to pull the orange into the bottle, it was only strong enough to grip it against the mouth of the bottle.

**Part 3:** Now say you've found a very interesting way of peeling a banana. Take the banana and peel the skin away from the top. Light another piece of paper, drop it into the second bottle and immediately invert the banana, pushing the peeled section into the mouth of the bottle. The flame will go out, suction will be created and, provided no air can get in, the banana will be stripped and disappear into the bottle. The children will find this great fun!

## And finally ...

Ask the children if they can find out a little more about vacuums and how they are used. No doubt they will quickly come back with information about vacuum flasks, which could be the basis for another session. With the help of their parents, they could also try the above experiment at home, perhaps using a soft boiled egg instead of a banana. With a bottle that has a neck only slightly smaller than the egg, and with a little judicious application of washing-up liquid to the egg, it is possible to get the egg into the bottle completely whole. Then ask the children if they've got any ideas for getting it out again ...

# CLEVER CUTS

## WHAT IS THIS ASSEMBLY ABOUT?

You show the children that they don't need expensive toys to have a lot of fun by creating beautiful paper patterns from a sheet of paper.

## WHAT YOU'LL NEED:

- Some sheets of A4 plain white paper
- A good pair of scissors – the large 'kitchen' type is best
- A pencil
- A large sheet of paper, approximately 60 x 60 cm – the paper should be very thin so that it is easy to cut when folded a number of times

## PREPARING THE ASSEMBLY

No preparation is needed for this assembly, but it's a good idea to have a waste paper bin handy to catch the little bits of paper from the cuts you're going to make.

Diagram 1

Diagram 2

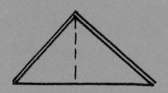

Diagram 3

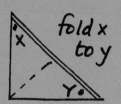

Diagram 4

# Introducing the assembly

**Part 1:** Tell the children that a surprising amount of fun can be had just with a sheet of paper and a pair of scissors. Show them a sheet of A4 and fold it in two lengthwise. Hold it folded edge downwards. Cut a triangle somewhere along the fold and ask the children if they can tell you what shape they will see when you open the paper up. They will find this easy and say a diamond or a rhombus.

**Part 2:** Take another sheet of A4 and fold it in half and then into quarters. Tell the children you want a square to appear in the middle of the paper but you're only going to make one cut. Ask them if they can suggest what cut you should make. Try some of the cuts suggested and show the children the results. When the right answer is suggested (Diagram 1), cut the paper and show them the square. Tell the children that interesting patterns can be created by folding and cutting – the more you fold, and the greater the number of shapes cut out, the more interesting the pattern. Fold another sheet of A4 into quarters and make the cuts shown in Diagram 2. Open up the paper to show the simple pattern that has been created. Now say you're going to try something a bit more ambitious.

**Part 3:** Take the large square of paper and fold it diagonally so that you have a large triangle as shown in Diagram 3. Fold along the dotted line indicated so that you create the right-angled triangle shown in Diagram 4. Fold point X to point Y along the dotted line to end up with the triangle shown in Diagram 5. Fold point A over to point B and you will have the shape shown in Diagram 6. Now draw in the shaded shapes shown in Diagram 7. Using your large kitchen scissors, cut out all the shaded bits and also cut off the end of the cone (line X,Y). Ask the children what they expect to see when you open the paper out. They will be surprised when they see the intricate and beautiful pattern you have created.

# And finally ...

Ask the children to experiment with paper folding and cutting and to try some different patterns and shapes of their own. They can also experiment by mounting their patterns onto different coloured and textured backgrounds. Perhaps they could bring their results into another assembly and show them to the other children. Following this, you can talk about simple origami patterns and show them some basic techniques.

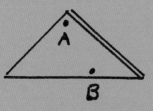

Diagram 5

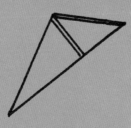

Diagram 6

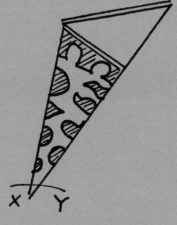

Diagram 7

# The Moving Coin That Doesn't Move

## What is this assembly about?

Light travels in straight lines, but you show how light rays can be bent to make three coins appear to move – even when nobody is touching them!

## What you'll need:

- Three 2p coins – bright, shiny ones are best because they can be seen more easily
- A shallow metal or plastic tray, about 40 x 30 cm
- A jug of water
- A tumbler
- A drinking straw
- Plasticine – optional

## Preparing the assembly

No preparation is needed for this session, but you will need to have a small low table at the front of the hall. Place the tray on the table.

# Introducing the assembly

**Part 1:** Ask a child to stand up (let's say his name is Charlie) and say 'Good morning' to everybody. Now ask Charlie to go out of the hall, walk along the corridor, around a corner and then shout out 'Good morning' again. Ask the children why we can still *hear* Charlie but we can't *see* him. Discuss the answers the children give you. Explain that sound travels in waves which can bend but that light travels in straight lines. Therefore, sound waves can travel around the corner, along the corridor, through the door and up to our ears, but the light waves can't go around corners or through things.

**Part 2:** Explain that it is possible to bend rays of light. Pop a drinking straw into the tumbler and fill it half full of water. Hold it up so the children can see that the bottom half of the straw appears to be bent. Explain that light rays fall on to the tumbler and its contents, and from there go to our eyes in straight lines, but that the water 'bends' the rays coming from the bottom half of the straw.

**Part 3:** Ask two children who are the same height to come to the front of the hall. Put the shallow tray in the centre of the table and place the three coins in the middle of the tray. It's a good idea to fix them in place with a little blob of plasticine. The children should stand next to each other, a short distance from the table. Tell them to edge forwards until they can *just see* the coins completely. Call this position 1. Now tell them to edge backwards until they *just can't see* the coins. Call this position 2. Very slowly, so the coins aren't disturbed, pour water from the jug into the tray. Before long, the two children will find the coins come into view again – even though the coins and the children haven't moved! Explain that once the children move back into position 2, light rays come from the coin but can't reach the children's eyes because the edge of the tray blocks them. However, in position 2 – once the water is added, the water bends the rays so that the coins appear at a higher angle and the children can therefore see them.

# And finally ...

Ask the children if they can find out about and experiment with any other examples of light bending or refracting. A very interesting example is the archer fish (or spinner fish), which can catch and eat creatures such as butterflies on the branches of river bank trees and bushes. It can not only shoot a spurt of water at an insect to knock it off the branch and into the water, but it also calculates the angle of refraction!

# ADDICTIVE ADDITION

## WHAT IS THIS ASSEMBLY ABOUT?

Maths puzzles can be great fun and very addictive. You start by showing the children a puzzle that tricks them and then demonstrate a very straightforward sum that *everybody* seems to get wrong!

## WHAT YOU'LL NEED:

- Some large sheets of A1 white paper
- An easel
- A bulldog clip
- A fat felt-tip pen
- Three calculators

## PREPARING THE ASSEMBLY

Very little preparation is needed for this assembly. Simply stand the easel at the front of the hall and fix the sheets of paper to it with a large bulldog clip.

# Introducing the assembly

**Part 1:** Tell the children you need three children who are particularly good at maths to come and help you. (The teachers in assembly can be asked to nominate them.) Give them a calculator each and tell them they can use it to solve the question you are going to ask. Draw the shape shown in Diagram 1 and say that it represents a little hole in the ground. Then ask, 'How much earth is there in that hole if it measures 10 cm wide x 10 cm long x 10 cm deep?' The children will probably perform a multiplication on their calculators and tell you the answer is 1,000 cubic centimetres. You then reveal that it's a trick question – because there isn't any earth in an empty hole!

**Part 2:** Write the number 192 on a second large sheet of paper. Ask the three children to add 3 to what you've written on the paper. Undoubtedly they'll tell you the answer is 195. Tell them you forgot to mention the rest of the question – that the answer must be less than 20. They will probably tell you it's impossible – until you explain that 1 + 9 + 2 + 3 equals 15!

**Part 3:** By this time, the children will be accusing you of not being strictly honest with your questions! Now tell them that you will ask them a totally straightforward sum, but you're certain they'll come up with the wrong answer. This time though they cannot use a calculator. Tell them to add together the following numbers out loud: 1,000; 20; 30; 1,000; 1,030; 1,000 and 20. If there are teachers in the hall, ask them to do it too. It's virtually certain that everybody will come up with the same answer – 5,000 – which is the wrong answer! When everybody seems really puzzled, write up the sum on another large sheet of paper, so the numbers can be clearly seen, and then add it all up.

## And finally ...

There are lots of excellent books on mathematical and geometrical puzzles and many activities online. Children are often fascinated by them. It's worth having quite a few puzzle books in school, as children very much enjoy trying puzzles on each other – and their teachers. They may also discover interesting ones that they can bring into an assembly on another occasion.

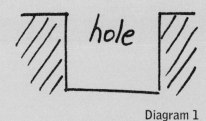

Diagram 1

# The Fearless Flyer

## What is this assembly about?

Using our senses, we can understand and interact with our surroundings – but take one sense away and everything goes haywire!

## What you'll need:

- A blindfold
- A plank, about 1.5 m long and 30 cm wide
- A small sturdy wooden or plastic box for the plank to rest on (to keep it above ground level)
- A marble

## Preparing the assembly

No preparation is needed for this assembly. Simply place the box at the front of the hall and sit the plank on it, so that the middle of the plank rests on the middle of the box.

# INTRODUCING THE ASSEMBLY

**Part 1:** Ask the children if they can name the five senses. Then explain how important all five are and how they enable us to understand our surroundings. Tell the children that if we lose one of our senses, the others are often heightened to compensate for the lost sense – such as the sense of touch in people who have very poor sight. Explain that when we lose a sense, we can also be easily fooled into thinking that something is happening which actually isn't, and that this can be very simply demonstrated using a marble.

**Part 2:** Ask a child to come to the front of the hall. Say that it's important that they can't see, so to achieve this you will be placing a blindfold over her eyes. Now ask her to cross the first two fingers of her right hand, leaving a little space between the fingertips. Put the marble into the small gap between the tops of the crossed fingers. Ask the child to tell you how many marbles you've put between her fingers. She will say two … because it feels exactly like two! Her brain is confused because she cannot see how many marbles there are and her fingers aren't in their usual position. Her brain therefore interprets what she feels incorrectly. Tell the children they can try this for themselves using any small object. It works very well on the round part of the nose, for example!

**Part 3:** Now ask if there is a small and very brave child who is willing to come to the front and help you. Undoubtedly you will have quite a few offers! You also need four older children, two of whom should be quite strong and the other two should be the same height and quite tall. The two strong children should stand at the ends of the plank and the other two children should stand one on each side of it, as shown on page 16. Ask the small child to go out of the hall for the moment so she can't hear what you tell the other children.

Now explain that when the child comes back in, she will be asked to stand in the centre of the plank and then be blindfolded. She will place her hands on the shoulders of the tall children standing on either side of the plank. The strong children at the ends will then start to lift the plank, but they'll stop at about 30 cm and then just gently wobble it to give the small child the *impression* that they're still raising it. *At the same time*, the children at the sides will gradually shrink down, so that the small child's hands are moving steadily downwards. The two children should stop moving downwards when the small child has to bend a little to try to keep her hands on their shoulders.

Now ask the small child to come back in. Stand her on the plank and put the blindfold on. Carry out the instructions above, and when the children at the sides are fairly low, ask the small child how high in the air she feels. She'll say, 'Very high!' The movement of the two children shrinking down, which she won't know about because *she* can't see it, and the fact that she *feels* her hands going downwards, will fool her brain into thinking she is travelling upwards. In fact, of course, she is only about 30 cm off the ground.

# AND FINALLY …

There are many ways of fooling the brain. Children find experiments with vision and sound, such as the one described, particularly interesting. Also, most children will be familiar with optical illusions because there are lots of books about them. Children might like to hunt out a few optical illusions in books or on the internet, work out how they fool the brain and then bring them in to show during another assembly.

# GIVE ME A RING

## WHAT IS THIS ASSEMBLY ABOUT?

This is a very old game that really makes children reason and think. It's usually played with a pencil and a scrap of paper, but the version you're going to make is ideal for showing in assembly.

## WHAT YOU'LL NEED:

- A piece of board approximately 50 cm square – a piece of brightly painted MDF is ideal
- Fourteen nails
- Fourteen rings – large wooden curtain rings are perfect because they need to be seen clearly by all the children
- A hammer

## PREPARING THE ASSEMBLY

Hammer the nails into the board as shown below, seven in the top row, five in the second and two in the third. The rings hang on the nails. The board needs to be supported (e.g. on an easel) at the front of the hall. Start the session using only the top row of seven rings. Remove all the others.

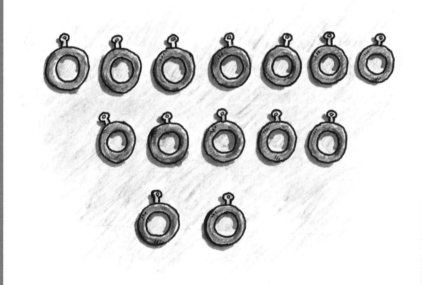

# INTRODUCING THE ASSEMBLY

**Part 1:** Tell the children that you're going to show them a game which seems very simple, but which actually becomes more *difficult* the better you get at it! Ask two children to come to the front to help you, and show everybody the board with the seven rings hanging on it. Explain that the idea of the game is to make your opponent remove the *last ring* from the board. The rules are simple. When it's a player's turn, he can remove one, two or three rings, but if two or three are removed, they *must* be next to each other. Ask the children to play. It will take only a few seconds for one of them to win. Let them try it once or twice more.

**Part 2:** Choose two different children (or a teacher and a child – children love beating their teacher!) and say you're going to show them the full version of the game. The rules are virtually identical and the loser is the child who removes the last ring. Hang all fourteen rings on the board.

The rules are as follows:

■ A player can remove one, two or three rings from any row.

■ The rings removed must be in the same row.

■ The rings removed must be next to each other.

■ Each player must try to force their opponent into removing the final ring.

# AND FINALLY ...

After playing for a while, the children will begin to think ahead, especially as the game nears its end, and they will start recognising certain patterns that could lead them to a win.

Does it make a difference who starts first? Is it better to go for bunches of two or three, or stick to single removals? Is it more advantageous to remove the rings on the edges of the lines, or go for the centre?

It really is quite addictive! Can the children find any other games which *seem* simple, but are actually more difficult than they look?

# SURPRISING SEVENS

## WHAT IS THIS ASSEMBLY ABOUT?

Using three dice, you make an amazing prediction – and then show how dice can be used for an interesting maths experiment.

## WHAT YOU'LL NEED:

- Twelve dice – it's a good idea to make some from wooden or plastic cubes so they can be easily seen
- Two sheets of A4 paper
- Six large sheets of white paper about A1 size
- Six fat felt-tip pens
- Masking tape
- Six containers to shake the dice in

## PREPARING THE ASSEMBLY

A little preparation is needed for this assembly. Stand the containers on a table at the front, along with the sheets of paper and the pencils. Write the number 14 on a sheet of A4, fold it up and put it in your left pocket. Write the number 21 on another sheet and put it in your right pocket. Draw eleven columns on a sheet of A1 and then write the numbers 2 to 12 at the top of the columns. Do the same with the other five sheets. Fix the sheets of paper at various points around the front of the hall using bits of masking tape. All the children will need to be able to see them.

# Introducing the assembly

**Part 1:** Explain to the children that people who really enjoy maths can find interesting mathematical ideas all around them, even using something as simple as dice. Say that the assembly you're going to do is based on the number 7. Now say that you're going to perform an amazing mind-reading trick, and ask a boy and a girl to come and help you. Tell everyone that you wrote a number on a sheet of paper before the assembly and hid it in your pocket, but you won't reveal what the number is for the moment.

Place two dice in a container, hand it to the girl, ask her to shake it and then roll the dice out onto the table. She should look at the two numbers showing on the top faces of the dice, then pick the dice up together and turn them over to reveal the two numbers underneath. She should then add the four numbers together. Ask her what her answer is. She will say 14. Now take out the sheet of paper on which you wrote 14 and show everyone how brilliant your prediction was!

Tell the children you're going to see if you can predict accurately again, but using three dice this time. Put three dice in a container and give it to the boy. Now the procedure is the same as before. The dice are rolled out onto the table and the top face numbers added to the ones underneath. Ask the boy what his answer is … and then take out your paper with 21 written on it. Amazing!

**Part 2:** Ask twelve children to come and help you, and explain that you're going to show them another interesting experiment with dice. Separate them into groups of two, give each pair two dice and a pen, and send each pair to a place where you've fixed a sheet of A1. One person in each group is the 'roller' and the other is the 'recorder'. Each pair works independently. Tell the children you're going to give them five minutes for this experiment and that they should work as quickly as possible. When you say 'Go', a roller should roll his dice on the floor, add together the two numbers showing and give the number to his recorder, who puts a tick in the appropriate column.

The more ticks you have on the sheets of paper, the better this will work. Everybody in the hall will watch the ticks building up with interest, and very quickly very similar patterns should emerge on all the sheets – with 7 being the number that appears with the greatest frequency. After five minutes, ask the children to quickly total the ticks in each column and then see if they can explain why this happens.

# And finally ...

Once children play around with dice, they will quickly discover that opposite numbers always add up to 7. Number 1 is underneath 6, 2 is underneath 5 and 4 is underneath 3. Using a pair of dice, numbers opposite each other will always add up to 14 (and so on), which is why you were able to 'predict' so accurately! In the second part of the session using two dice, there are more ways of making 7 with them than any other number, so this is the number most likely to appear when you roll the dice.

# ALTERNATIVE ART

## WHAT IS THIS ASSEMBLY ABOUT?

You don't necessarily need a paintbrush and a pot of paint to create an interesting picture. You show three alternative ways of creating some fascinating artwork very quickly.

## WHAT YOU'LL NEED:

- An iron, heated to a medium setting
- An easel to show your work
- Some fat wax crayons of various colours
- A pair of scissors
- A sheet of white sugar paper, A3 size
- Two sheets of white cartridge paper, A3 size
- A bulldog clip
- A small pot of mild bleach
- A thick white candle with the wick cut off
- A pot of ready-mixed water-based paint – any colour will do
- Some non-permanent blue writing ink
- A few paintbrushes, one fairly thick

## PREPARING THE ASSEMBLY

You will need a small table with a wipe-clean surface. Some of the work will be done on here and some on the easel. You will need a bulldog clip to hold the paper on the easel. Well before the session, paint a couple of sheets of white cartridge paper with the blue writing ink.

# INTRODUCING THE ASSEMBLY

Explain to the children that art is great fun, and that although most people enjoy experimenting with paper and paints, there are lots of other ways to create pictures too. Tell them that you are going to show them just three because these can be demonstrated in a very short space of time.

**Creating picture 1:** Show the children a sheet of paper that you have 'painted' using blue ink and clip it on the easel. Then hold up the small container of bleach and explain that the liquid, although it looks just like water, can create a picture by removing the ink wherever the brush touches it. Dip a brush into the bleach and draw a very simple picture with it. The children will be surprised to see a 'negative' picture appearing as if by magic. Then put the other sheet on the easel and ask a child to come and have a go. (You might want to add that bleach is corrosive, so care should always be taken when using it. It is a good idea if the child painting with the bleach wears plastic disposable gloves.)

**Creating picture 2:** This time say you're going to create a picture without drawing or painting on the paper at all. Fold a sheet of white sugar paper lengthwise, unfold it and lay it on the table. Next, using the blade of the scissors, scrape off little pieces of wax from a thick wax crayon and let them drop on the left hand side of the paper. Do the same thing with three other colours, always keeping the bits in the left hand area. Then use your finger to rearrange the coloured scrapings so they are spread out in an interesting pattern. Fold the right hand side of the paper onto the scrapings, taking care not to disturb the pattern, and carefully iron the paper for a short while to melt the wax. When the paper is opened, an attractive symmetrical pattern will be revealed.

**Creating picture 3:** Clip a sheet of white cartridge paper onto the easel and draw a picture using the candle tip, pushing on the candle as hard as you can. The children will not be able to see what you are drawing because the streaks of candle wax will be invisible from a distance. When you've created an interesting sketch, give the sheet of paper a wash of colour using the small pot of paint. As you paint over the paper, the picture will appear like magic because the wax resists the colour!

# AND FINALLY ...

Tell the children that although you have given them three ideas, there are hundreds more to be found in art books and that artists experiment with all kinds of media and materials. Even spreading watery paint onto paper and then blowing at it through a straw can produce very interesting results. There is plenty of scope here for looking at the work of various painters and sculptors in other assemblies too.

# Squashed Tomatoes

## What is this assembly about?

Any spelling game that makes spelling fun is worthwhile. You demonstrate a simple one that teachers will probably want to play in their classrooms too.

## What you'll need:

- Cut out some comic squashed tomatoes from pieces of red card – you will need about ten of them
- Masking tape
- An easel
- Some large sheets of white paper
- A fat felt-tip pen

## Preparing the assembly

The preparation for this assembly is very simple. Make some small coils of masking tape and fasten a coil to the back of each squashed tomato. Lay all the squashed tomatoes on the table at the front, masking tape upwards.

# Introducing the assembly

Playing the game: The object of the game is simple: just avoid getting any squashed tomatoes! You get one if you complete a word. Get three and you're out of the game!

Explain to the children that you're going to show them a spelling game that is good fun and can be played anywhere by two or more players. Ask four children to come to the front. It is best if these children are good spellers so the game is demonstrated effectively. We'll call them child A, B, C and D.

Child A thinks of a word. He doesn't say it, he just calls out the first letter. Let's suppose he's thinking of the word 'part' and calls out P. Write a P on the easel paper so that everyone can see it. Child B tries to mentally guess the word child A is thinking of, and then he calls out what he thinks is the second letter. As there are lots of words beginning with P, he may think, for example, that the word is 'post', so he calls out the letter O. You then write an O on the paper so that all the children can see the word building up.

Now child C tries to imagine what the word is and she calls out the next letter. She might think the word is 'pore', in which case she'll call out R. Now it's child D's turn to guess the fourth letter. She might think the word is 'port' and call out T. You write it down – but everyone can see that by adding a T, child D has *completed* a word. She therefore gets a squashed tomato stuck on her. Now child D has to think of a new word, give the first letter, and it's then back to child A for the next letter. The game carries on until one child has earned three squashed tomatoes for finishing off words, in which case he must leave the game. The other three continue until just one player emerges as the winner.

Here's a reminder of the rules:

- The winner is the child who doesn't acquire three squashed tomatoes.
- As soon as a word is completed, the child who added the last letter gets a tomato.
- Children should be encouraged to keep the game going by using longer words, although it is easy to get caught. A child might have been trying to keep things going by thinking of 'cardigan', but as soon as the R has been reached, a word has been spelled!
- Words must be two letters or more.
- A child can challenge the previous child if he suspects that an incorrect letter has been added or the player is bluffing and is just adding any old letter. If so, then the previous player has to say what word he was thinking of, and if wrong, he gets a tomato.

# And finally ...

By using children who can spell well, the game can become very exciting, especially when most of the players have two squashed tomatoes. It will also encourage other children, who might have lesser spelling skills, to have a go. Children in the main part of the hall must be encouraged not to call out or give any clues to the players! It is best to limit the amount of thinking time each player has. You might also want to give the winners a prize!

# LIFTING THE LID

## WHAT IS THIS ASSEMBLY ABOUT?

The air all around us is odourless, colourless, you can't feel it or taste it, and it's invisible. But in this session, the children learn some facts about air when you make it perform three interesting tricks!

## WHAT YOU'LL NEED:

- A metal tin with a tight fitting lid (a very large coffee tin with a smaller centrally fitting lid is ideal)
- A small camping gas burner
- Matches
- A metal tripod (or similar) – the tin sits on top of it and the burner goes underneath
- A balloon
- A reasonably large paper bag
- A pin
- A small hammer
- If possible, a few colourful pictures of dramatic lightning storms

## PREPARING THE ASSEMBLY

There is very little preparation for this assembly, but as it has an 'explosive' element safety precautions need to be thought about. The large tin and its lid will become hot, so have a cloth handy to pick them up after the experiment.

# Introducing the assembly

**Part 1:** Ask the children to tell you some facts about air and have a short discussion about it. Then say that, although we can't see it, air can certainly make its presence felt. Blow the balloon up slowly and knot the neck. Push the pin into the balloon and ask the children why it goes bang. Discuss their answers, and then explain that when air suddenly moves quickly, such as when it's rushing out of a popped balloon, it hits the surrounding air with force and large violent sound waves are created which travel to our ears. Demonstrate the idea again by blowing up the paper bag, twisting the top and then exploding it with your other hand.

**Part 2:** Go on to talk about thunder and lightning. Explain how lightning heats up the air, causing it to expand extremely quickly, creating a similar violent reaction with the surrounding air. It's a good idea to have some colourful pictures or diagrams available to illustrate this part of the assembly.

**Part 3:** Explain that you're now going to show just how hard air can push when it's heated. Pull your table back, as far away from the front row of children as you can. Show the children the large empty tin and ask one child to push the lid on the tin firmly so that no air can escape. To do this, he can tap round the edge of the lid gently with the small hammer. It mustn't be too tight. The child should then go and sit down with his class. Stand the tin on the tripod, light the gas burner and slide it under the tripod. After a short while the tin lid will be fired into the air with a loud pop. Explain that as the air becomes hotter it expands and looks for the weakest part of the tin, which of course is the lid. For safety, note that it is very important to try out this experiment beforehand, so that you know just how high the lid will go.

# And finally ...

There are, of course, many other fascinating experiments with air which are very suitable for demonstrating and talking about in assembly – for example, air pressure or the way in which our bodies use air. Following this assembly, the children might like to search for more information about air and then show their findings later on in the week. Or perhaps each class could find an experiment about air and demonstrate it in assembly to all the other children.

# So Who Am I?

## What is this assembly about?

This is a simple game that the children will want to play in class once they've seen you demonstrate it in assembly. When playing it, the children have to think carefully and devise rapid, relevant and logical questions.

## Preparing the assembly

No preparation for this session is needed other than making some very simple hats.

## What you'll need:

- Some 'hats' for the children. These can be simply strips of brightly coloured card, about 10 cm wide, stapled together to make a headband. Alternatively, you could make something a little more fancy, as shown in the illustration. The number you make will depend on how many classes of children are in the hall – if there are six classes, make six hats.

- A fat felt-tip pen

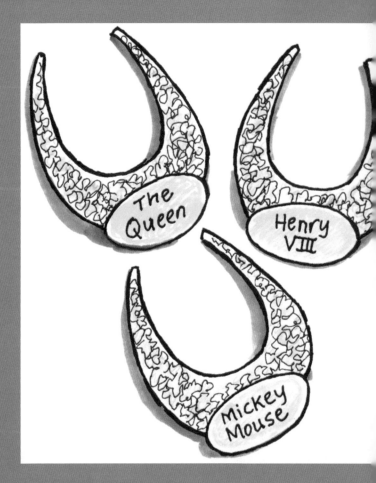

# Introducing the assembly

**Part 1:** You will need one child from each class to volunteer to play the game. They should all stand at the front, facing the rest of the children. Ask child 1 to go out of the hall, so that he can't hear what is being said. Now ask the children in his class to give you the name of a well-known real or fictitious character. Somebody might say, for example, Mickey Mouse, so you write 'Mickey Mouse' in large letters on the first hat. Ask the child to come back in, and put the hat on his head with the character's name pointing towards the front. It is important that he doesn't see the name or work out who he is, so everyone else must keep very quiet.

Tell child 1 he has three minutes to discover who he is. He can ask his class any questions he likes and the class must answer his questions accurately but briefly, without giving away too much information. He should obviously ask his questions as rapidly as possible to make best use of the time and narrow the options. He could start with, 'Am I alive or dead?' 'Am I male or female?' 'Am I human or non-human?' 'Am I old or young?' 'Am I a famous TV star?' and so on.

After the allotted time, if the child hasn't discovered who he is, show him the name on his hat. You can then begin the same process with the next child and that child's class.

**Part 2:** If children are guessing their identities fairly quickly, and they probably will, you could play a harder version of the game in which the child can ask his class questions but they are only able to answer 'Yes' or 'No'. So the child could no longer ask, 'Am I female or male?' but must ask, 'Am I female?' This version of the game takes longer, so you wouldn't be able to give as many children a turn.

# And finally ...

There are countless variations to this game, and you could narrow the field to just choosing the names of people who play sports, characters in films or on television, or famous fictitious characters from books or poems. It's also great fun if a few teachers are willing to come to the front and play the game. This will greatly amuse the children – and the whackier the characters chosen, the funnier they will find it!

# SOUND SENSE

## WHAT IS THIS ASSEMBLY ABOUT?

This assembly is all about how sound waves travel. You show how we can pinpoint the direction of sounds and the way sound changes when funnelled through different shapes. And then you communicate with a child quite a distance from the hall – using a piece of string!

## WHAT YOU'LL NEED:

- A ball of string
- A pair of scissors
- Some sheets of A1 sugar paper
- Two polystyrene or thin plastic cups
- A cardboard tube – the longer the better
- Some masking tape
- A CD player and a CD of Beethoven's Ninth Symphony
- A blindfold

## PREPARING THE ASSEMBLY

Very little preparation is needed for this session. Simply punch a small hole through the bottoms of the cups and you're ready to take the assembly.

# Introducing the assembly

**Part 1:** Tell the children you want them to listen carefully to a piece of music. Play them a short piece from the choral section of the Ninth Symphony. Then ask them to imagine what it must have been like for Beethoven never to have heard his wonderful symphony due to his deafness. Explain how he had to be turned around to face the audience because he couldn't hear them cheering.

We take our hearing for granted and yet the way sound reaches our brain is remarkable. Ask two children to help you – we'll call them Tom and Sadie. Tom should stand at the back of the hall, in the centre, facing towards the front. Blindfold Sadie and stand her at the front, facing all the children. Ask Tom to say 'Hello' in a fairly loud voice. Then ask Sadie to point to where the voice is coming from. Ask Tom to move and then call out again. Do this several times. Each time Sadie will be able to pinpoint exactly where the 'Hello' is coming from. Explain that having two ears enables us to do this; if Tom is standing to the right, his voice (sound waves) will reach Sadie's right ear *fractionally* before her left ear, therefore she knows he's on the right.

**Part 2:** Ask Tom to return to the front of the hall. Give him the long cardboard tube and ask him to hold it up to Sadie's ear and speak softly into it. His voice will be surprisingly loud to Sadie because the sound waves are concentrated in the tube. Roll a large sheet of paper into a fat cone, making the sort of ear trumpet that Beethoven used to carry around (in a pram!). Ask Tom to put the narrow end in his ear and show how it improves his hearing because it 'collects' a lot of sound. Reveal how it improves even further if he has a cone in each ear.

**Part 3:** Explain that sound can travel along and through materials as well, and that you're going to demonstrate this with a piece of string and two plastic cups. Push the end of the string through the hole in the bottom of one cup and make a knot so that it can't come out. Ask Tom to walk with the cup to the other end of the hall (or preferably out of the hall and along the corridor, provided the string can be kept in a tight straight line). Now cut the string, push the other end through the second cup and tie a knot. Keep the string taut. Sadie should now hold the cup and speak into it, while Tom listens in his cup, making sure he puts the mouth of the cup firmly over his ear. Sadie's words should be quite clear to him.

Call Tom back and ask him what Sadie said. Then reverse the roles, sending Sadie down the corridor. Explain that the vibrations from our voice travel along the string. The string 'telephone' works surprisingly well, even over quite a long distance, and the children should find this very interesting to watch.

# And finally ...

It is a good idea to follow up this assembly with another on the story of the Frenchman, René Laennec, who invented the stethoscope after watching children transmit sound through a wooden beam by scratching it with a pin – rather like the cardboard tube effect in the session described above. Interesting experiments can be done in another session on the beating of the heart and how the sound of it can be heard by doctors listening through a stethoscope. It hasn't really changed much since Laennec invented it!

# A Pressing Problem

## What is this assembly about?

This session is about the power of air. You show that, although we don't normally feel the weight of the air around us, it can actually push very hard!

## Preparing the assembly

Push the lid firmly onto the tin, and then punch a hole through the centre of the lid with the hammer and nail. Turn the tin over and punch a hole in the bottom, opposite the top hole. Put a plasticine plug over the bottom hole.

## What you'll need:

- A pair of scissors
- A round balloon and a 'sausage' balloon – the bigger and longer the better!
- A toilet roll tube
- Some sticky tape
- A small metal tin with a tightly fitting lid
- A hammer
- A nail
- Some plasticine
- A bowl
- A jug of water
- About 15 metres of string

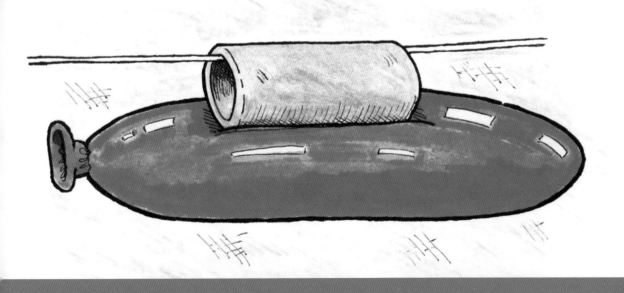

# Introducing the assembly

**Part 1:** Talk about air and its properties. Tell the children that, although they don't feel its weight, air is surprisingly heavy. Ask five children to come to the front. Tell child A to stand in front of child B and gently push his chest. Child B will move backwards. Explain that air pushes against us, just like child A pushed against child B, but we don't normally feel its force because air is pressing equally from every direction. Illustrate this by having child A push against child B again, but with child C pushing B's back and D and E pushing from the sides. They should all try to push gently but equally. Child B will stay still because the pressure is equal.

**Part 2:** Show everybody the tin, and the fact that you have plugged the small hole in the bottom with plasticine. Take the lid off the tin, hold it over the bowl and fill the tin with water. Put the lid on the tin, hold it upright over the bowl and ask the children what will happen when you take the plasticine plug away. They will probably say the water is heavy and that it will come out through the hole. Take the plug away but keep your index finger on the hole in the *top* of the tin. The water doesn't come out! Ask if they can explain this 'pressing problem'. If they can't, explain that the air is pushing on your finger, rather than pressing on the surface of the water and encouraging it through the hole.

**Part 3:** Show the children the round balloon, blow it up and let it go. Explain that the force of the air rushing out of the balloon makes it whizz all over the place, but if you control the direction in which the air pushes, a simple rocket can be made using a tube and a ball of string. Blow up the sausage balloon as far as it will go. Ask child A to pinch the neck to stop the air coming out, while you sticky tape the cardboard tube to the middle of the balloon. Thread the string through the tube and ask child B to hold the end of it. Ask child C to take the other end of the string and walk to the other end of the hall. The string must be stretched tautly. Ask child A to release the neck of the balloon – and the balloon will shoot along the string!

# And finally ...

There are many aspects of air which make fascinating things to talk about and demonstrate – for example, the movement of air and the effects of high winds. Interesting work can also be done on kites and parachutes. With a little careful planning, you can even talk about what happens when air is heated and demonstrate how a hot air balloon works!

# Puzzling Paper

## What is this assembly about?

Using just a pair of scissors and some pieces of paper, you demonstrate that the impossible is possible and the possible impossible!

## What you'll need:

- A good pair of scissors
- Ten pieces of paper measuring approximately 5 x 20 cm
- Three sheets of A3 paper
- A piece of paper the size of a postcard

## Preparing the assembly

The preparation for this session couldn't be simpler. Simply take the ten smaller pieces of paper and cut two slits in each one, as shown in Diagram 1. The slits should be of equal length.

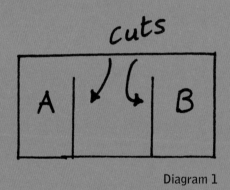

Diagram 1

# Introducing the assembly

**Part 1:** Ask for ten children to come and help you, five boys and five girls. Stand them in a row facing everybody, with the boys standing separately from the girls. Give each boy one of the pieces of paper with slits. Explain that you are going to give them an extremely easy task to do – it really couldn't be easier – but you bet they can't do it. In fact, if any of them can do it, you will give that person a big bag of sweets! Ask the boys to hold up their pieces of paper, grasping section A in their left hand and section B in their right. Now ask the first boy to pull hard and equally on sections A and B, so the middle bit of paper falls to the floor.

The first boy will try and be unable to do it. Ask the second boy to have a go with his piece and he won't be able to do it either. Let the other boys try. None of them will be able to pull the end sections of their papers so that the middle piece falls to the floor. Now turn to the girls, give each of them a piece of paper with the slits and explain that they are *bound* to be able to do it because they're so much cleverer than the boys! Once again, none of the girls will be able to do it – because it's impossible. The brain is wonderfully clever but it simply cannot make both hands pull equally. Your bag of sweets is safe! (Although you can always give them to the children for helping.)

**Part 2:** Ask four children to help you. Give the first three children a sheet of A3 paper each. Hand the first child a pair of scissors and ask him to cut a hole in the paper big enough to put his finger through. He'll do it easily. Hand the scissors to the second child and ask her to cut a hole in her sheet of paper big enough to put her arm through. Again, it will be easily done. Now ask the third child to cut a hole in his sheet of paper big enough to put his head through. Child 3 shouldn't have any difficulty either.

Now hand the postcard sized paper to child 4. Explain that you've only got this piece of paper left, but you want her to cut a hole in it big enough to put her whole body through! Naturally, she'll say it is impossible, and all the other children will undoubtedly agree with her. Then you show them how it's done. Fold the piece of paper and cut where the dotted lines are shown in Diagram 2. Then snip the folds marked in bold lines. When you open out the paper you will have a large paper ring big enough to walk through!

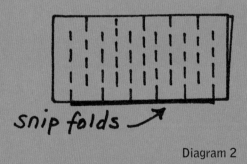

snip folds ➔

Diagram 2

## And finally ...

Children are fascinated by demonstrations like this because they appear almost magical, and there are lots of books and online content containing similar ideas. Optical illusions are always fascinating, too, and an excellent session can be done on simple Victorian optical toys and illusions which confuse the eyes and are fun to watch.

# WHACKY WORDS

## WHAT IS THIS ASSEMBLY ABOUT?

Words are fascinating. We use them all the time to communicate, but lots of fun can be had with them too, as this session demonstrates!

## WHAT YOU'LL NEED:

- An easel
- Some large sheets of paper
- A bulldog clip
- A thick felt-tip pen

## PREPARING THE ASSEMBLY

Another very easy assembly to prepare. Just fix the sheets of paper to the easel with a big bulldog clip and you're ready to start.

Diagram 1

NEVER ODD
OR EVEN

Diagram 2

TOM WHERE FRED
HAD HAD HAD HAD HAD HAD HAD
HAD HAD HAD BEEN THE CORRECT
ANSWER

Diagram 3

# Introducing the assembly

Talk to the children about words. Explain how important they are for communication, how we use them all the time and how very young children quickly acquire large vocabularies at a startling rate. Tell the children that words can also provide endless fun, and that you're going to show them some word puzzles and ask them some questions that will really test their thinking powers.

**Puzzle 1:** Ask a child to come and help you. Tell him that, however hard he tries, you're going to catch him out! Ask if he can spell the word 'silk', giving you the letters one at a time. Write the letters on the paper. Now ask him to spell out what a cow drinks. He will spell the letters of the word 'milk', and be certain he was right. You point out that a cow makes milk but actually drinks water!

**Puzzle 2:** Ask another child to help. Tell her you're going to draw a well-known vegetable on your paper and all she has to do is guess what it is. Draw the picture shown in Diagram 1. She will probably be completely mystified, until you explain that the word is 'potatoes': a cooking *pot* containing *eight* letter *O's*!

**Puzzle 3:** Write the sentence 'Never odd or even' on the paper, as shown in Diagram 2. Ask the children if they can spot something interesting. There will be all sorts of answers until somebody notices that it's a palindrome – it says the same thing forwards and backwards.

**Puzzle 4:** Here's a tough one. Write out the sentence in Diagram 3, 'Tom where Fred had had had had had had had had been the correct answer,' and ask the children if it makes sense. They will say, of course, that it doesn't. Could it ever make sense, you ask? They'll say, no, it couldn't possibly. But you can show that it does! Explain it like this: Tom and Fred were in class, copying down a sentence the teacher had given the class. The sentence was, 'Everybody had had so much jelly, they felt ill.' Tom didn't copy it down properly. He wrote 'Everybody had so much jelly, they felt ill.' Fred, however, *did* copy it down properly. And so Tom, where Fred had had 'had had', had had 'had'. 'Had had' had been the correct answer.

# And finally ...

There are thousands of amusing tricks and puzzles with words, many of them fascinating to children. Once you've shown them the palindrome above, for example, they'll probably want to construct a few themselves. A whole session could be given over to crosswords, their invention and construction. The internet is a very rich source of word puzzles too.

# TANTALISING TABLES

## WHAT IS THIS ASSEMBLY ABOUT?

Look deeper at any times table and some very interesting things come to light. The 9 times table, for example …

## WHAT YOU'LL NEED:

- An easel
- Some large sheets of paper, clipped to the easel, to write on
- Ten sheets of white card, about A4 size
- A thick black felt-tip pen
- The largest calculator you can find, or an electronic whiteboard

## PREPARING THE ASSEMBLY

Take the first sheet of white card and write 1 x 9 = 9 on it, as large as possible. Take the second and write 2 x 9 = 18. On the third write 3 x 9 = 27, and so on up to 10 x 9 = 90 on the last card. On the large sheet of paper fixed to the easel, write the number 12,345,679. (Note that the number 8 isn't included.) You're now ready for the assembly.

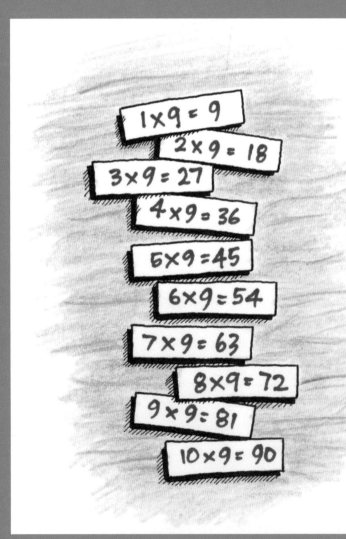

# Introducing the assembly

**Part 1:** Talk about times tables, why we learn them and how useful they are to us. Explain, for example, that if you're working out area or volume quickly, knowing your times tables makes everything that much faster. Show how knowing your times tables can be useful to a decorator, a carpenter or a carpet fitter. Then say that people interested in mathematics have a great time playing around with numbers and that times tables can be a fascinating place to start. Explain that you're going to take the 9 times table as an example, and ask ten children to come to the front and help you. Stand them in a row facing everybody and give each child one of the ten cards, in the order of the 9 times table. Initially they should only show the blank sides of the cards.

Ask everybody to say the 9 times table out loud. The children at the front should turn their card over when the children get to the number showing on their card. Now ask all the children to look carefully at the *answers* only, and ask if anybody can spot something interesting about them. The digits in each answer add up to 9!

**Part 2:** Now explain that the 9 times table is one of the easiest to learn. Ask the children to look at the answers on the cards and see if they can explain why. Then show that all the numbers on the left hand side of the answers go *up* in sequence from 0 to 9, and all the numbers on the right hand side of the answers go *down* in sequence from 9 to 0.

**Part 3:** Ask another child to hold the calculator, or to go to the calculator in the whiteboard software. Point to the number you've written on the easel (12,345,679), which consists of the numbers 1 to 9 but with the 8 missing. Ask the child to type this number into the calculator and multiply it by the first answer in the 9 times table (9). The result will be a long string of 1's. Ask the child to multiply the number by the second answer in the 9 times table (18). The result will be a string of 2's. Now multiply it by the third answer (27) and you will have a long string of 3's. And so on. If there's time, find out what happens if you add the 8 into the first number, and what happens if you reverse the big number.

# And finally ...

Children in primary school spend a lot of time exploring aspects of mathematics, such as geometry, and numbers can be just as fascinating. All sorts of interesting things can be found just by drawing a tables grid and looking at the patterns that emerge. Some could be prepared for a future assembly. Exploring numbers using a calculator can be fun too. You don't have to work it all out in your head!

# MUSICAL MAYHEM

## WHAT IS THIS ASSEMBLY ABOUT?

You show how some simple musical instruments can be made from everyday objects, and you create an instant band!

## WHAT YOU'LL NEED:

- For the box bass: a large and very stout cardboard box, a broom handle and some thick string

- For the rice shaker: a small tin with a lid and some rice

- For the tumbler xylophone: eight identical tumblers (or mugs) and a metal teaspoon

- For the straw clarinets: four drinking straws and a pair of scissors

- For the water trombones: two bottles, two short lengths of plastic tubing and some water

## PREPARING THE ASSEMBLY

Prepare the box bass. Drill a hole through the broom handle, about an inch from the top. Thread the string through and tie a knot so that it won't come out. Turn the box upside down and drill a hole through the bottom, about two inches from the edge. Push the other end of the string through the hole and tie a knot. When the broom handle is held upright on the upturned box, the string must be taut so that it can be plucked.

# Introducing the assembly

**Instrument 1:** Hold up an ordinary school recorder, play a few notes on it and show that it is basically just a tube with holes, which when covered up move the air in different ways to produce a range of notes. Explain that most musical instruments are based on simple principles. Ask nine children to come out and help you. Ask child 1 to hold the tin while you pour some rice in. Push the top on tightly and then ask the child to practise some simple rhythms by shaking it.

**Instrument 2:** Place the tumblers in a row, put a little water in the first, a little more in the second and so on, until by hitting them with a metal spoon you can produce a scale. Label the first one 'C', the second 'D' and so on. To save time, you will probably want to try this out well before assembly and then mark the tumblers so you know how much water to pour into each one. Explain that the notes change depending on how much room there is in the tumbler for the air to move around. Child 2 is going to play this 'instrument'. It helps if she is fairly musical and could try, 'When the Saints Go Marching In'. Here are the notes for it: CEFG, CEFG, CEFGECED, EEDCCEGGF, FEFGECDC.

**Instrument 3:** Show how you have made the box bass and explain that it works by plucking the string at various points, which vibrates the box and the air beneath it. The range of notes will be restricted but ask child 3 to have a go. He should put his foot on the box to steady it and practise holding the broom handle firmly upright and the string fairly taut.

**Instrument 4:** Take the four straws and at the ends of each, pinch about 1 cm flat. Cut off the edges of the flattened sections so that triangular shapes are left. Give them to children 4, 5, 6 and 7. Ask them to put the straws a little way into their mouths and blow hard. With a little practice a sound will be produced. Now, by pinching the straws at various points along their lengths and using a pair of scissors, cut some tiny holes, three in each straw. Again, with some practice and by covering some of the holes, the children should be able to make a small range of different notes. It isn't easy though, and some will be better at it than others, which is why it's a good idea to have four or five players for these straw clarinets!

**Instrument 5:** Pour water into the two bottles until they are about three-quarters full. Place the pieces of tubing into the bottles. Ask children 8 and 9 to hold the bottles in their left hands and the tips of the tubing in their right. Now they should blow across the top of the tubing until they get a sound. Then, by moving the bottles up and down they can change the notes, and even get a 'slide' effect as the air moves through shorter and longer sections of water-free tube. Explain that a trombone works in this manner.

# And finally ...

Now the 'band' should be ready to play. If the child on the tumbler xylophone plays 'When the Saints Go Marching In' and the other children join in by blowing, plucking and shaking with enthusiasm, it will certainly produce an interesting noise! It also helps if a teacher can play the piano or the guitar to make it all a bit more tuneful!

# DECORATIVE DIFFUSION

## WHAT IS THIS ASSEMBLY ABOUT?

You show how to create an interesting picture using a drinking straw, a few coloured paints and a toothbrush.

## PREPARING THE ASSEMBLY

Fix one of the large sheets of white paper to the easel with a bulldog clip. Unscrew the top of the garden sprayer and fill it a third full with some diluted paint. Screw the top back on. Now you're ready to start the assembly!

## WHAT YOU'LL NEED:

- Some small pieces of thin card
- A pair of scissors
- A glue stick
- An easel
- Some sheets of white paper
- A bulldog clip
- A drinking straw
- A plastic paint pallet
- An old toothbrush
- A small square of stiff card or plastic
- A flower sprayer – the sort that can be bought for a couple of pounds in a garden centre
- Some small pots containing ready-mixed paint, but with added water to make the paint flow easily – three or four colours will be enough

# Introducing the assembly

**Technique 1:** Show the children the garden sprayer and unscrew the top. Explain that by pumping the handle, air is brought into the sprayer. It pushes on the liquid and forces it up the central tube, where an adjustable nozzle with different sized holes can create a very fine spray. This can be used to create an interesting picture. To demonstrate this, take several of the small pieces of card and cut each one into a shape. Put a dab of glue onto the stencils and arrange them on the white paper on the easel. Now, using the finest spray setting, spray some paint over the paper, leave it a minute or so, and then pull the shapes away to reveal the picture.

**Technique 2:** Explain that the picture would be much more interesting if you emptied the colour from the sprayer, filled it several times with different colours and then sprayed some more. But that would take time. Say that you can do a similar thing with just an ordinary drinking straw and a few small pots of coloured paint. Put a new sheet of paper on the easel, take another piece of card and cut a stencil – for example, you might try the shape of a house and cut out some windows and a door – and then lightly stick the stencil onto the paper.

Take the drinking straw and, about a third of the way from the end, cut almost through the straw but not quite. Bend the straw into a right angle at the cut and push the short end into a small pot of diluted paint held in your right hand. Keep the cut about a quarter of an inch above the surface of the liquid. Supporting the straw in your left hand, and aiming at the stencil on the paper, blow hard through the long section. Paint will come out through the slit as a spray. Explain that it works in the same way as the garden sprayer, but this time you're using your mouth as a pump. Spray using the other coloured pots of paint as well to create an interesting picture and then remove the stencil.

**Technique 3:** Tell the children you can create a similar picture without pumping any air at all. Set up a fresh sheet of paper, cut out another simple stencil and fix it to the paper as before. Squirt several colours of paint into a pallet, but don't add any water because they need to be thicker for this technique. Now dip the toothbrush into one of the paint colours, loading the bristles thoroughly. Hold the toothbrush near the stencil and then, using the small thick piece of card or plastic, draw it *backwards* across the bristles. This will cause the paint to fly forwards, and with a little practice it will be just like a fine spray. Dip the toothbrush into some water to clean it, dry the bristles and do the same thing with several other colours before lifting the stencil away from the paper.

## And finally ...

Although it's nice if children are asked to come to the front to try a little spraying or toothbrush artistry for themselves, they need to wear smocks or aprons as things can get a little messy. For example, if a child pushes the small piece of card forwards instead of pulling it backwards across the toothbrush, she could spray herself instead of the stencil!

# ANIMATED ANTICS

## WHAT IS THIS ASSEMBLY ABOUT?

If we didn't have the phenomenon known as 'persistence of vision', cinema and television wouldn't exist. You explain it and demonstrate three different ways of illustrating it.

## WHAT YOU'LL NEED:

- A short length of broom handle
- A piece of very stout corrugated card, about 35 cm square
- A hammer
- A nail
- A pair of scissors
- A strip of white card approximately 8 x 40 cm – paint one side of the card black or glue a piece of black paper onto it
- A piece of stiff white card, about 10 cm square
- Red, yellow and black large felt-tip pens
- A new pencil
- Two large elastic bands
- Some sticky tape

## PREPARING THE ASSEMBLY

Firstly, you need to make a simple turntable. Draw the largest possible circle on the corrugated card and cut it out. Hammer a nail through its centre and into the end of the broom handle. Don't hammer it right in – the disc needs to be able to spin. Take the strip of white card and cut slits into it, as shown in Diagram 1. Then draw the 'stick man' sequence onto it, as shown, each image being slightly different from the last. Take the small piece of stiff white card and draw a large red blob on one side of it. On the other side, draw a large yellow blob. Finally, punch two holes at the sides of the card, thread the elastic bands through and tie them so they won't come out.

# Introducing the assembly

**Part 1:** Ask the children to stare at a light bulb in the hall for a short time and then shut their eyes. They will still 'see' the image. The image 'persists' for a short time. Take the pencil and hold it up in the air, gripping it about a third of the way along using your right hand finger and thumb. Hold it very loosely. Now waggle it up and down and the pencil will appear to be bending, as if it was made of rubber (you'll need to practise a little to get the right effect). Our eyes see it in the up position, but before it can register on the brain, it's moved to the down position, and then up again and so on. Our eyes can't keep up with the movement. Explain that when we watch a film at the cinema, it is really a series of still images, each slightly different from the last. Because the images change quickly, our eyes can't keep pace, so the images seem to combine and we think we see a moving picture.

**Part 2:** A similar effect can be demonstrated using the card with the elastic bands. Ask a child to hold the ends of the elastic bands and pull a little to stretch them. Show that there is a different colour on each side of the card. Now 'wind up' the card by turning it over and over until it won't turn any more. Let it go, and because our eyes can't keep up with what we're seeing, the colours seem to combine, making the blob appear orange.

**Part 3:** Show the turntable and how it spins on the nail. Curl the stick man strip into a circle, fastening the ends with a piece of sticky tape, and sit the strip on the turntable. Ask a small group of children to come and stand with you. Tell them to look through the slits at the stick man pictures as you spin the turntable. As they watch, the man's arms will appear to go up and down. Explain that this was a very popular Victorian toy called the zoetrope, and there are still versions of it on sale today. One is shown on page 44.

Diagram 1

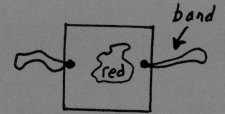

Diagram 2

# And finally ...

Obviously, only a small group of children can observe the effect in your home-made zoetrope during this session, but it can always be sent around to the classes afterwards. Many children will probably be encouraged to make their own as it isn't very difficult. There are also many other persistence of vision experiments to be found in books and on the internet.

# SERIOUS STRENGTH

## WHAT IS THIS ASSEMBLY ABOUT?

You show that a surprising amount of strength can exist in something that seems rather weak – and vice versa!

## WHAT YOU'LL NEED:

- A table
- A very large sheet of newspaper – a double-page spread from a Sunday paper is perfect
- A ruler
- Some stiff corrugated card
- Some ordinary thin card
- A large circular biscuit or cake tin
- A sheet of A4 paper
- Two tumblers
- A few rolls of masking tape
- A piece of 12 mm plywood (or similar) about 30 cm square

## PREPARING THE ASSEMBLY

Cut a length of corrugated card the same height and length as the perimeter of the cake tin. Fix the ends together with strong glue or masking tape so that it won't come apart. Now do the same thing with a strip of ordinary thin card. No other preparation is needed for this assembly.

# Introducing the assembly

**Part 1:** Ask two children, a boy and a girl who think they are very strong, to come out and help you. Also ask a small child to come out and join them. Ask the two strong children to take turns in lifting up the smaller child and praise them, saying that yes, they do seem to be very strong! Now place the ruler on the middle front edge of the table, two thirds of it on the table and the other third hanging over the edge. Ask what would happen if you hit the hanging part very hard. They will say the ruler would fly up into the air, which it would, of course.

Now lay the sheet of newspaper on the table, so that it covers the ruler, but not the section that hangs over the edge. Explain that the newspaper is very light. Ask them what would happen now if you hit the hanging part very hard? The children will either say the ruler and the paper will fly into the air or that the paper will split. Ask the girl to hit it as hard as she possibly can and then ask the boy to try. Neither the paper nor the ruler will move, however hard they try! Tell the children they weren't as strong as they thought – but then explain that the air pressure on the large surface area of the paper prevents the ruler moving!

**Part 2:** Place two tumblers upside down on the table, about 20 cm apart, and place a sheet of A4 paper across them. Ask the children if the paper is strong enough to support one or two rolls of masking tape placed on top of it. They will naturally say no. Pick up the paper, fold it backwards and forwards into thin strips, as if you were going to make a fan, and balance it across the tumblers again. Okay, you cheated a bit, but the sheet of paper will now support quite a few rolls of masking tape!

**Part 3:** Ask a small child to come to the front to help you. Place the biscuit tin on the floor and place the piece of plywood on top of it. Ask everybody what will happen if the child stands on the piece of wood. They will undoubtedly say that the biscuit tin is strong enough to support him. Demonstrate that they were right. Now ask what would happen if you removed the biscuit tin and replaced it with the circle of thin card. They will say that the card would collapse.

Now explain that card *can* be strong enough to support a heavy weight, and show the children a piece of corrugated card. Peel it apart to reveal the strong, fluted inner layer, similar to the folding you did with the A4 paper, and explain that this section can give the outer layers a great deal of strength. Demonstrate this by putting the circle of corrugated card on the floor, placing the wood on top and asking the child to stand on it. His weight can be supported easily. The card was a great deal stronger than the children thought!

# And finally ...

This assembly can lead on to a further interesting one showing how packaging materials which *seem* very light and fragile can actually give great protective strength – for example, polystyrene foam and balls, bubble wrap and air-filled plastic pouches. It can be great fun testing out different kinds of packaging to see if a box can be knocked about without the contents being damaged!

# Tension Tricks

## What is this assembly about?

Although it can't be seen or felt, you explain that, just like us, liquids have a skin – and then you prove it by showing the children three experiments with water.

## Preparing the assembly

Place a chair at the front, beside your table. Stand the tumbler on the table and fill it two-thirds full of coloured water. So that it can be seen easily you may want to stand it on a small box. As these experiments could be difficult to see clearly from a distance, you may want to seat the children nearer to you for this assembly.

## What you'll need:

- A large transparent dish or bowl of water
- A tablespoon
- A tomato
- Some washing-up liquid
- A tumbler
- A jug of coloured water (dilute a little paint into it)
- Three matchsticks
- An elastic band
- A milk bottle or similar
- A small square of gauze or mesh

# Introducing the assembly

**Part 1:** Ask a younger child (we'll call her Sally) to come and help you. Stand her on the chair. Hold up the tomato and ask the children if there are any differences between Sally and the tomato. The children will find this amusing and will point out lots of differences!

Then ask if they can think of something that is the *same* about Sally and the tomato. It won't be long before somebody points out that both Sally and the tomato have a skin. Now explain that, surprisingly, liquids have a skin too, even though you can't see it as easily as the skin on a vegetable, fruit or human being.

**Part 2:** Show the tumbler with the coloured water. Now gradually add more coloured water to it until the tumbler is full. Ask the children if it's possible to fill it any further and they'll say no. Continue adding water very carefully with the spoon until it just starts to drip over the side. Ask Sally to get down to the level of the rim of the glass, and she'll be able to see quite clearly the convex shape of the water skin.

**Part 3:** Place the bowl of water on the box so that it can be seen clearly. Drop the three matchsticks into the water, in a triangle shape as near to the centre of the bowl as you can, so that they float. Explain that the water skin, or surface tension, is supporting them. Now let a tiny drop of washing-up liquid fall into the triangle. The three matchsticks will suddenly spring apart. Explain that soapy liquid destroys the surface tension, which is why washing-up liquid helps to get dishes clean quickly. It breaks down the surface tension and allows the water to get closer to the dishes.

**Part 4:** Fill the bottle full of coloured water, right up to the brim, and then stretch the gauze over the top, keeping it secure with an elastic band. Ask the children what they think will happen if you turn the bottle upside down. They will undoubtedly say that the water will trickle out through the holes. Turn the bottle over quickly and show that the water *doesn't* pour out, because the skin of the water around all of the little mesh holes is keeping the water inside.

# And finally ...

Apart from these experiments, which children can easily try for themselves at home, there are many other variations on the surface tension theme. Instead of the matchsticks, a loop of thread can be dropped into the water and the washing-up liquid will cause it to form a circle. A small cork dropped into a tumbler of water will quickly float to the side, but fill a tumbler until the skin forms a convex surface and the cork will settle in the middle as it finds the highest water point.

# Dedicated Discussion

## What is this assembly about?

This is a fun session in which children watch a short playlet and then debate the issues raised afterwards.

## What you'll need:

- Four children to play Mrs Cheesecake, her little boy Charlie, Constable Catch 'Em and Billy Burly (Billy should be older and taller than Charlie)
- Some dressing-up clothes for the characters
- A satchel containing a brightly coloured fizzy drink, a bar of chocolate, a packet of crisps and two biscuits
- Large sheets of paper with questions (see note at the end of the playlet)

## Preparing the assembly

If it can't be prepared beforehand, the actors can read the parts of the following short scene. At the start of the assembly, they should be waiting outside the hall or room where you're doing the assembly.

## Introducing the assembly

Tell everyone they're going to watch some children perform a short scene, and they must watch carefully because you will be asking some questions afterwards. Mrs Cheesecake now comes in and hurries across the hall, holding Charlie by the hand. Charlie carries the satchel. Billy is in hot pursuit. Mrs Cheesecake turns to Billy and they act out the following dialogue:

Mrs Cheesecake: Oi! What do you think you're doing? You just leave my little boy alone.

Billy: I wasn't doing anything Mrs.

Mrs Cheesecake: Yes you were. You were trying to take my little Charlie's satchel. I saw you and you saw him, didn't you, Charlie?

Charlie: Mum, I …

Mrs Cheesecake: You see? I shall summon a policeman. Look, here comes one now. (*Constable Catch 'Em enters from the other side*)

Constable Catch 'Em: Now then, now then, what's all this fuss?

Mrs Cheesecake: Officer, I'm Mrs Cheesecake and this very naughty boy was trying to take my little Charlie's satchel. Wasn't he, Charlie?

Charlie: Mum, I …

Billy: I wasn't doing anything, honest. I was just …

Mrs Cheesecake: You see? Guilty as anything! Take him away and lock him up, officer. (*She takes the biscuits out of the satchel*) These biscuits are my Charlie's lunch, aren't they Charlie?

Charlie: Mum, I …

Mrs Cheesecake: Be quiet, Charlie. And this boy is trying to take them. Arrest him right now!

Constable Catch 'Em: Two biscuits? Is that all he's having?

Mrs Cheesecake: No, of course not. Do you think I'm trying to starve my little boy? Look, he's having a bag of crisps as well.

Constable Catch 'Em: So he's just having two biscuits and a packet of crisps?

Mrs Cheesecake: No, look, I've got him a bar of chocolate for his pudding.

Constable Catch 'Em: So, let me get this right … he's having two biscuits, a packet of crisps and a bar of chocolate?

Mrs Cheesecake: No, I've got him this nice fizzy drink as well.

Charlie: Mum, I …

Mrs Cheesecake: Pipe down, Charlie, the constable's talking. You see, officer, my poor little boy nearly didn't have any dinner at all because this very naughty boy was trying to take it. Clap him in irons and give him three years' community service!

Billy: All I was trying to do was tell him his shoelaces were undone. I didn't want him to fall over and hurt himself!

Charlie: Mum, I …

Mrs Cheesecake: Be quiet, Charlie, you've got far too much to say for yourself.

Constable Catch 'Em: Hmm. Well, all these sensible children here have been watching, and I *shall* have a word with this young man. And I think I need to have a little word with you too, Mrs Cheesecake …

The children will have fun watching this playlet. Next, get the actors to hold up some sheets of paper with questions on that will start a short discussion, such as 'What might Constable Catch 'Em say to Billy?' or 'What might Constable Catch 'Em say to Mrs Cheesecake' or 'Why wasn't Mrs Cheesecake a very sensible mum?'

## AND FINALLY ...

It takes only twenty minutes or so to write a simple little playlet for a few children to act, and if a session like this is done occasionally, all sorts of dilemmas and issues can be introduced. The discussions need to be short and tightly focused – they can always be followed up in depth later on in the classroom.

# A Final Thought

An assembly is such a valuable time for a school leader and the children. I hope this book has not only given you a great deal of enjoyment and a range of promising assembly themes, but has also sparked lots of ideas of your own.

Some of the most successful assemblies I've done have been almost spur of the moment. Sorting out her loft one Sunday, a member of staff found a 1930s phonograph. It was complete but in pieces. We had a wonderful time in assembly on Monday morning gradually putting it back together while the children tried to guess what it was as it took shape.

On another occasion, after seating five members of staff on a bench, I challenged a tiny infant child to lift up the bench. The children all said it was impossible – and then, to their great amusement, I introduced the car jack I'd been using before school started, put it under one end of the bench and the infant pumped it up with ease! This led to a discussion on other amazing machines and how they work – the crane, for example, which was being used on a housing development opposite the school.

Young children have a real thirst for knowledge and an endless fascination with the world around them which we, as teachers, need to nurture. And it can start in a lively and fascinating school assembly …